AF560507

Catharsis

Catharsis

Selected Poems By

MUKUL KUMAR

Title: Catharsis
Author: Mukul Kumar

ISBN: 978-93-92210-77-8
Edition: I

Published by:
JGS Enterprises Pvt Ltd
Imprint: The Browser

Publisher's Address:
SCO 14-15, FF, Sector 8-C, Chandigarh 160 009
Website: thebrowser.org
Email: service@thebrowser.org

Printed in India

Editing, Layout and Cover Design by beagles
99beagles.com

Dedicated to Lord Shiva

Contents

Acknowledgements

First and foremost, my family: my parents, my wife, and my little daughter, who have always been, visibly or invisibly, by my side encouraging me on through my literary journey. Khushi Ram has extended valuable support during the editing. I am grateful to my Service for all the possible support to realise my creativity. And last but not the least, I owe special gratitude to Sahitya Akedmi *(Indian Literature),* Sukrita Paul Kumar, The Times of India, The Hindu, and The Indian Express for praising the book.

Mukul Kumar

Mr. Das

A seamless mass of people is
swarming out at this peak hour,
It is the majestic Victoria Terminus;
Mr. Das has been picked out of it.

Mr. Das winds his way through the shifting
barricades of shoulders and elbows-
the vacuum amidst them is clogged;
Man has multiplied to be too close
for sight and speech.

Mr. Das is immaculate in his dress,
Clean in his habits,
Discovers a clean foothold
even amidst the densest of squalor;
Vortex in living doesn't ruffle him.

Earlier, he had emerged from
his apartment-a tiny cell in a High-rise
draped in despair by the brackish air of Mumbai,
into the basement to pick his scooter;
He had hurried himself for the
Nominated suburban service;
The tryst with the time.
Now, he paces up to haul himself
into the elevator;
He enters a door that beams a woman,
her shining teeth emanant in the foreground;

It is the corporate office of a
toothpaste manufacturing company,
He will lose himself into the files-
soft and hard, to retrieve his mortgaged identity.

Mr. Das navigates the consuming chores,
but is still connected with the world;
A citizen of the global village-
distances have disappeared into waves and wires.
Filling up the vacuum is instant;
He chirps through the tiny chip,
Talks with his hands clicking the mouse,
Hears with his ears plugged.

Silence is paramount;
No sound should drown
the hum of the air conditioner,
as it sucks the warm air out;
In this office, words die on the tongue,
smiles on the lips.

The day-end is struck;
Tomorrow is already snaking
upon the dying day;
He chugs into trail for tomorrow.

Mr. Das stands squeezed
into the stillness of the racing train,
his refuge calling him aloud;

Over the yesteryears, the sight passing by
has been seen blank-
The fragments of the sky struggling through
the electrical wires and sky rises,
The shanties by the side,
A horrific harmony.
Mr. Das will not be fazed by
the accidental fall of a man, or
the lacerations of a woman by
the lascivious eyes and twitching hands;
These tangents will spoil the
circle of his existence.

Home; the day is dead;
Now the rendezvous with the
flat faces beamed by Television;
They fill the vacuums interspersed between
the wife's regular errands and
his son's homework.

Ultimately, he will invoke sleep to
blow out his mind;
At the appointed hour,
by the automatic command of habit,
it will be switched on again.
He finds himself again perched at
the first dot of the circle.

The Beggar

A beggar
Limbless,
Armless.
The fragments barely clad,
The begging bowl tied to
one of the arms;
He rolls over the pathway
along the Garments shops, and
stomachs out a cacophonous score;
His voice is getting drowned into
the clatter of stones raining into
his empty bowl.

A Dahlia of Forty-Five

Nature never comes to me in surfeit,
Even a transient, tranquil stare at
a flower, a croton, or a creeper,
comes to me as a wondrous treat.

As the spectacles that meet my eyes,
And the actions that find my hands,
Day in and day out, threaten me
With a sense of hubbub and humdrum,
Nature promises an instant wonder,
The surreal immanent in the real,
The prodigious in the prosaic;
A costless access to the soul,
as it swifts through the wearied eyes.

Hence, the winter breakfast in my lawns,
wallowing in the wrap of the warm Sun;
It has told me the life cycle of the
Dahlias, to lucent flames from spawns.

The vision effects my gaze cast
upon a senile dahlia, discoloured,
its petals wrinkled into a gloomy mass,
it is just about to part with the plant.
I am swung into a curious melancholy.

A sigh escapes, ah not long it will last!
The vision shifts from youth to infirmity,
My gaze turns frantic, sweeping along
the row of the flowers, myriad and motley;
I Search for the Dahlia that perfectly pairs
with a man of forty-five.

The Journey Without Destination

The night is set ablaze;
I am on the beach,
witness to the sea extinguishing
into the rippling sky,
the starless firmament;
The sky above, the sky below,
The monochromatic sphere,
The mirage rises realised;
The vision is witness to solitude,
that wanders on the forlorn beach.
It is grappling with the void without.

Back in my room;
Spell of the blazing night lingers on;
The world beyond the window box,
has collapsed into mere contours;
The window glass mirrors
the contours colliding with the
reflection of my fluorescent room;
Too convoluted for clarity;

Vision swivels in to seek the within,
surface is ever elusive;
It's a bottomless fall,
The tantalising maze,
Cognition eludes.

I am grappling with the void within,
The voids, without and within,
pair up in resonance;
An eerie euphony-
This journey has no destination.

When I Was My Mother's Son

The night of pain;
Frenzied fever,
Fuming forehead;
Lurks the hand that caressed the
head that housed a mind
ignorant of disease, but aware-
the hand was the talisman that would
weave a convalescent sleep;
One of the many apparitions that
split this sleepless stupor tonight.
Oh, the multiple hands of
the disease-dose knowledge
fail to stitch even a refuge of oblivion.

Life; a Fatuous Frenzy

I am the volume,
transfigured out of the ether,
to thrive in this garb.

Set afloat is the buoyant garb,
the force and fury
known in the child in
possession of the cherished.
It unfurls itself, a sensuous smugness,
displaying its colours and contours,
amassing pride and plaudits;
A frenzied venture.

Alas if this fatuous frenzy were
just not an ephemeral import,
sucked back to replenish the reserve;
It is the frenzy of the Whole for
sporting identities!

Epiphany

I will attain what I want,
No matter umpteen hurdles there to daunt;
I have the will and wherewithal,
Have I ever suffered any withdrawal?

I am an ardent practitioner of Dharma,
Believe destiny to be the function of Karma;
I set off with my usual élan,
Sure that I am not a flash in the pan.

I try but fail,
I try again, but only to fail,
I try again, and again, and again,
But this time all the trials go in vain.

Am I too wearied, is the die cast?
I am frustrated, all downcast;
I question my philosophy,
Scan my belief for the anomaly.

I am plunged into entropy,
Is Karma the function of destiny?
I am caught up in the anomie,
Invoke the supernatural to rescue me.

I am tossed into transcendence,
Blessed with the tongue is the essence,
'Existence is not explained by absolute philosophy,
Finally, I glow up with the epiphany.

Fever

I am fevered,
I burn,
I groan,
Eyes half-shut;
An apparition lurks,
I melt,
Go wet,
Revel in the cooling sensations;
Dehydrated, yet my thirst
is sumptuously quenched.

They ask: why?
I reply: 'you'.
It is you, who sublimated into fever,
It is you, who melted back,
It is you, who fumed out;

You are the fever,
You are the saviour,
You are the odour.

The odour lingers on
Till it is washed off
as I bathe in the worldly waters.

The Death Not Mummified

Life is no more a celebration;
The sky is dimming,
The waters are flattening,
The earth is sighing,
The air is gasping,
Man is bemoaning man.
The unchanging environs have cast
an irredeemable monotony,
an impregnable gloom;
Change is hopelessly waiting to happen.

The gloom demands giant's grit;
Let fortitude ignite the fire,
Adventure is antidote to adversity;
Wonders of the World
may work wonders.
The pyramids of Giza first –
The celebration of death,
amidst the unending desert;
I find the pyramids heaving,
I am filled with a surreal horror;
Razing down will reveal the suspense;
Oh, life wafts out of the Mummies!

Perhaps, the impregnable gloom
has been cast by the
decadence from the mummified life.

My Blood Weaves a Magic

(My Little Daughter)

The stream of her gaze springs from
the reservoir of innocence sublime,
thaws the frost of opacity,
dissolves the shield of survival,
quickens my heart into the pulsation ordained.

Her gleeful, frenzied engagement
suffuses with meaning what is
shorn of sense to the experience,
redeems me out of meaning-
imputed or latent,
purging me of the pollution of existence.

Her tender touch upon my skin
transmits the nameless sensations,
entrancing me into a celestial cocoon;
I am blessed with a vain aloofness,
that integrates my split mind, and
embalms my unslept eyes.
Ah, how impassioned gets my zeal for life!

Lyric

Lyric is an edifice;
It is erected with the moments
mined from the quarry of time with
the spade of the suffering heart,
The syllables ordered in the pensive mind,
The tune orchestrated with sighs.

To the world it goes as a melancholic note,
Sweet and dulcet as a cuckoo remote,
But sung by the mechanical throat,
Lipped and re-lipped and yet remote.

But to me, no grudge, no pain, no shock,
There is nothing to make me mock,
For my song is profiled on my rock,
Why of my sufferings others to take stock!
Now happens the other way round,
Their pleasure is to my pain bound;
This makes my sinking heart sound,
Never letting my moments be mound.

This has made my tragedy sublime;
My hemlock to them is lemony and lime.
Pleasure from sorrow is permanent joy,
That enables me to take devil as toy.

My Shadow Salvages Me

Knowledge is not light, always.
I grope amidst the
walking luminous shadows,
Too dazzling for the knowledge of
colours; darkness tailored to
drape the multiple identities
in a single shadow;
Duplicity is the path-paver
for the trail to the top.

I look down upon my shadow,
Swung into the sport of sculpting light,
I fashion the myriad shadows of
my single identity;
Sure of the grey of head, and
the red of heart,
I rejoice at the ground;
I am salvaged by the smugness
from the instant cognition of the
shadows flickering flat beneath!

Shadow

My contour has slipped out of me,
It flickers flat on the Earth;
A stranger meets my eyes.
I want to trample this
earthly emanation beneath.

It eludes my steps as
I charge upon it,
slipping away, and away;
I am subjected to the existence
on the coordinate plane;
I end up oscillating along
the invisible hypotenuse.

My Garrage

The maid of my house
Lives in the house of my car;
My car exists
Because I have a house;
Her house exists
Because I have a car.

Aquarium

This is the house of glass,
A captivating floating mosaic,
The bed of Pebbles, Shells and Corals,
The entire sea squeezed in;
It is a specimen to my
keen aesthetic sense, and
the size of my heart.

My Lord Shiva

The trauma of travelling through the slum;
I am rendered grim and glum,
I fret and fume and fight,
But only to blight my plight;

The light of my life dimming,
For succour, I turn to Him, screaming,
The desperate feet of the soul rushing,
A turgid tide of tears gushing.

The surging hope affords a flushed interior,
I am resurrected with the eternal elixir;
Revealed to me is the vision of a seer,
Distilled only through tribute is this elixir.

Writer's Block

Nothing written for long!
Self-abnegation fills in;
The self is overcast with
a repentant gloom.

I will break the ice today itself,
thoughtless though I am;
The sensibility will serve again,
and thoughts will bloom.

Oh long minutes fly by,
Thoughts elude, mind a rebel;
A writer I am, the swagger sizzles,
but the void booms.

Nipped long, the swagger subsides;
'A writer you are, not by yours,
but nature's will'.
Large a thought finally looms.

The Poet Rebukes the Bureaucrat

The All India Writers Meet,
I am invited to recite my recent poems;
It's long since I have written any,
I feel enthused to write one.

I come back home from office,
Finish the evening sooner,
Hurry my way into the bed,
hungry for the solitude;
I extinguish the light to
illuminate the poet within;
But it's to no avail.

I try harder and harder,
But the poet remains eclipsed;
Frustrated, I wail-why,
The past invocations were all smiles;
The night is wading, wakeful,
The time is a terrifying translucence.

Lastly the poet pities me,
Ranting it rises,
"I remained long unvisited,
I even came uninvoked,
a divine flash that I am,
But you ignored my knocks,

I got eclipsed beyond your invocation;
Don't you know, bureaucrat and poet
are as apart as Antarctica and Arctic?

The poet continues its reproach,
'I am a creature with
A surging heart,
An untamed mind,
A spontaneous consciousness,
And free lips;
I recollect in tranquility the overflow,
The feelings in their spectral hues,
And tell them to the world
With an echoing symphony.

'And you are a bureaucrat,
A monolith, a monochrome, with
A draped heart,
A moulded mind,
A cultivated consciousness,
And tailored lips;
Well trained in the
Art of *stoicism* and *status quo,*
you are immune to the overflow;
Cap your feelings,
controlling the cup and colour,
and tell them to the world
with a calculated confidentiality.
Not only did you ignore me,

But abandoned me in the forlorn,
like an expired currency,
shifting to fiction for men and matter.

'Tonight, no gifting you a poem,
I can only thrust into you this dirge;
Sing it to the world to rescue poetry –
The art of
squeezing sea in a saucer,
universe in an urn;
That is a power divine,
wielded with the
serene soul,
seething sensibility,
sizzling sentiments,
wondrous words,
magical metaphors, and
resonating rhymes.

Applause you may amass,
singing this dirge;
Thus may return to poetry
the drifting poets-
the divine messengers
on this earth.'

Serenity Silenced

Not always man and nature resonate.

The silvery sky,
The swinging boughs,
The sonorous patter,
The luminous hue,
The blooming green,
The ether sublime.

Growth, Development, Evolution,
Religion, Art, Politics –
All are haunted by
The chimera of belief,
The crisis of faith;
Ah the tormenting tumult!

Trapped between the selves split,
Simmer the sighs-
Surged in the heart,
Articulated in the mind,
Expressed on the tongue, but
Dead on the lips.

No more rains the life;
Serenity no more is lent to
the rains lashing around.

It Is You

When you were here,
You were with me.
Now, you are gone,
You are within me.

My senses have transcended the body
to sense another self;
It is you.

My consciousness sculpts an image,
my emotions colouring it;
It is you.

I see what you saw,
I utter what you uttered,
My silences reverberate
with your sounds,
I am surrounded with
the multiple images,
They constitute one being;
It is you.

I have come to feeling tormented,
I am letting another self rule mine,
my world lies besieged,
all that was mine doesn't remain mine;
Fills in hatred for the ruler;

It is you.
But it's not long before
My excruciation meets epiphany,
It's a divine whisper-
'Finest love shows up in hatred only.'

Kargil

The deadening, cold, white crust;
A colossal expanse of winding sheet
sheathes the martyrs,
They died fighting over the line of split;

No volume of hot blood and breath
could thaw this impregnable crust,
Story after story,
a frozen history is the only crux.

Earth looks eerie, anointed with blood,
Sun is paled due to the extinguished life-fire,
Moon paints nature in the mourning white,
Humanity is trapped in the political quagmire.

The silence resounds with the muted cries,
The air feels heavy with the gris gloom,
I ponder over this debris of Civilization –
War is the act of the sane or loon?

History fuels the power-juggernaut on,
1947 replayed in 65, 71 and now 99;
Several such plays still imminent,
For the stitch in time saves nine.

Kashmir

On this exhibited miniature
I could not appreciate
the pristine brown of the earth,
the exquisite blue of the waters,
the sublime green of the flora,
the celestial azure of the sky,
recreated to perfection;
I also see the translucent red film,
that is smeared all over,
but is missing from the frame.

The Confession of a Bigot

I have the head that
can exorcise the hunger;
Now my head is shaken by
the ever-thickening storm of hunger;
To be a master sorcerer,
I have practised history,
History never fails at hypnosis;
The gorge of hunger is
inverted upside down,
It is bound to ignite the hearts
of the hapless hungry,
The ensuing fire will form
the halo that will legitimize my head.

Silence Is Not Peace – 26/11

…Threat,
Fear,
Agony,
Blood,
Scream,
Silence.

Silence, silence and silence …….
It explodes into screams,
but to be wearied into silence,
yet again.

Silence is not always peace,
'Sanity in silence' is no more affordable;
Stares into the face the specter of
the incessant stream of screams.

History has witnessed creations
seeded into cataclysms;
Let the voice be bestowed
at once,
that pronounces peace,
not silence.

The Naini Lake

On the terrace of the retreat,
that verlooks the Naini lake,
I sail for winged hours on a few
moments of our past togetherness;
Every iota of the ether filled in
the cup of the lake and mountain
reveals the boating duo that
peopled that togetherness.

You Make Me a Seer

In this moment of thaw,
enveloped in a silvery hue,
drenched in a cathartic glee,
I ooze thee.

Love's flash illuminates my
conscience and character;
Such an absolute revelation!
I always believed transfiguration
was accessible only to a seer,
and that too not before
the years of rigour.

The Fisher Boy

His circulation rages over
The blood oozing out,
His embroils are in turmoil
over the embroils he is extracting,
His integrity is lacerated
by the slices littered down.

His gaze retorts my perception–
'There brews a storm in the gulf
between my sight and your vision,
This, you live beyond, and
I live within.'

The Street Acrobat

He walks with his hands,
upside down,
his head stirred by shame;
But his inverted intestines
coil around his head, and
steady it in balance.

Blind to the audience,
he navigates meticulously;
Even quite a while hence,
he notices that he is navigating
only over the concrete,
and no currency;
In not long,
he watches a horde of intestines
furiously leaping out from
the undifferentiated bodies;
They flog him back upon his feet.

My Moon Is Lost

The silvery hue from
the radiant moon!
But it no longer dispels the
darkness over inner horizon.
Alas, if my moon were
not blown out by
one ambitious head, and
two strong feet!

The Residue

As I wrestle with the tentacles in
my stomach,
I intently look at the blue enema
placed on the window in
my front,
and also, lying next to it
my head
that contains the grey potion,
as I wish to wrestle with
the tentacles in
My heart.

Loneliness

Can you decipher the silence
Abuzz with the unspoken words?
Can you smell the presence
of those who are absent?
Can you understand the language
the creases of my bed speak?
Can you read my mind
from the impressions over my pillow?
Can you map the doors
embedded with my eyes?
Can you discern on the walls
the unreal friezes I see?
Can you estimate in my intoxicated eyes
the blackness of the night?
Can you scale the incarcerated ambitions
my yawns fume out?
Can you catch from my ears the
cacophonous breaths reverberating therein?
Can you discern night
my morning carries?
Only then can you measure my loneliness!
Only then can you measure my loneliness!

Afternoon

A still, hot afternoon,
Phlegmatic,
Yawns melting in the eyes,
An inadvertent slumber,
The senses stupefied,
A distant bark of a street dog
amplifies the silence,
foments the stillness.
The Sun barges through the slits,
sits in the shapes myriad,
precipitates a tenebrous translucence,
smudges the vision.

A malicious melancholy,
A melee of apparitions,
A canvas is concocted,
A silhouette stretches out to
slip into the portrait there on;
It retreats in despair.

Now this afternoon pervades
throughout the day;
It has found home
in my slumberous mind.

She Dies of Starvation

Wrinkles wrought not by age,
but dripping desires and drives,
Despair dried in the eyes;
It is the deluge of the drought that
has drowned the fleet of the fathers,
she has ordained to nurture her;
But she hunts for the food to live on.

Forlorn in such a fatherless recess,
She eats the mango seeds and dies;
So, her God owns her hungry,
despite the bursting godowns.

The worms that her wrinkles house,
also swarm the godowns;
They reconcile God owning her hungry
to the Godowns being hers.

These worms have swallowed
the distinction between
the nation of surplus food grains, and
the nation of surplus lives.

Cremation

The grieving kin's scream
amplifies the deathly silence,
It reverberates in the corridors
of the government hospital.

Release the body,
I will cremate it,
God has to be propitiated to
precipitate the peace of the soul.

Police is yet to arrive,
Procedure is long and
Formalities are galore, and
Ambulance is still awaited,
Don't lose patience for
the peace of the patients,
Counsels the doctor
with tact and poise.

The kin's anxiety is smothered,
He sits forlorn on the visitor's bench,
his head reconciled, but heart in revolt,
throat teary, but eyes in fumes;
Loneliness rests in a crowded corner.

His words have been engulfed by
a haunting thought-
what has been cremated for the
peace of the bodies moving around?

By Chance

Science and chance;
A contrarian stance?

Science theorises-
the singularity exploded into infinity
with a Big Bang;
Earth, Sky, Moon and Sun,
A perfect order in a flash sprang;
The single cell multiplied to be man;
But didn't life charge the cell
by chance?

Science claims,
the universe is a design;
But didn't the interglacial Holocene
make way for earth and humans, and
wasn't the earth's spin delicate for the
right heat and water for the life,
by chance?

Hence, man discovered fire,
killed animals, made weapons,
ploughed earth, grew crops,
melted irons, devised technology,
tamed nature, created resources;
Leaped from survival into surplus;
Conceived beauty, created art,

crafted the human civilization;
I am a smug citizen of this civilization.
But how long will the Holocene last?
Is civilization a timed transience?

At night the question hits,
as darkness illuminates the soul.
May I live to witness the apocalypse?
Man is cracking gene to conquer death,
I seek assurance from science,
It retorts-you live still
by chance.

Wearied between science and chance,
the subconscious rises to weave a trance;
The apparition is my Shiva;
Thus spoke He-
It is only the victory of death
that can never happen even
by chance.

I wake up, steeped in the surreal,
and for sanity rush into the
trail of living;
The belief burgeons-
Science is the progeny of Chance.

The Habit of Living

The emptiness emanates from
the frozen frame,
It fills my heart.
The chantings bemoan the absence,
the invocations throated out by the
perspiring priest mellow the
seething stillness into hollow motions-
the choreographed cores.
The habit of absence rises
before the absence sets in.

I Have Created

The cauldron of creativity,
the ashes of life lived reduce to
the infancy.
This infant lies huddled to my
newly born daughter.
The duo depicts the fusion-
the pleasure of procreation, and
the contentment of creation.

An Uncategorised Moment

The afternoon siesta leaves me
adrift, yet anchored;

Visionless gazes,
Mindless thoughts,
Motionless journey.

This lifeless moment effects
the climax of life;
Life is born of the muse – 'Life.'

A Wet Sight

The soft breeze,
The singing boughs,
The silvery ether,
The cloud-shot sky – a celestial collage,
The symphony of the pattering rains;
I am driven into a tremulous freeze.

The vision illuminates what
the sight cannot afford,
Shadows the memory mundane,
Shrouds the reason earthen.

The blessed drops upon tremulous leaves;
Destiny makes teeming pearls
out of the formless volume.

Out of breath's slotted measure,
I crave for the destined moments-
The pearls for my treasure!

The Old Man and Me

The old man walks gently,
I jog briskly;
The contrast is double-edged.

His aged heart transmits the
tautness of his limbs
to the stick he walks with-
support to the being he is.
.

My young heart transmits the
tautness of my limbs to
the being I am not.

My Pitiable Pity

The clouds of an overcast self
will never rain;
They are torn asunder by the
ever-expanding skies of
avarice and ambition, and
hemmed by the
fire in the furnace;
They churn out incessantly the
new foods to fuel up
the hunger in the well-fed belly.
How pitiable are the
Clouds of my pity!

Funeral of My Faith

I waded through the debris,
My wearied self was fuelled
by the last vestige of faith.
Faith is burnt, fuel is over,
I am left to drag the sail that is
sinking under the weight of values;
The harbours around are
too silted to anchor the
boats with deep bottoms.
Alas, the values live in death only,
before they are calculably lived as
the function of time!

Spring

Every spring,
the tree in my garden
sheds the dry leaves;
It is anticipation of the new.
Alas, if the tree of time
could shed the dry moments
in anticipation of the future!

The dry leaves turn into humus,
and rise again as leaves to live
till the ensuing spring.

One solitary spring,
this tree of time had shed
a few moments that rise as life,
today;
An eternal spring is engendered.

I Have Lost an Arm

A glance at the man at bus-stand,
I sense my being gathered into
the hollow sleeve of his shirt;
Its nothingness is all-pervasive.
I wriggle to wrest my being back,
lest I am left not merely a spirit,
without the body.
But it retorts-
I have lost one arm, and
now I cannot enter the body
with two arms.

I Meet the Horizon

Horizon is a mirage,
seen but never met.
I run into it,
beholding the burst of
the clouds over the setting sun.
One August evening,
I meet the horizon within,
Witness the burst of the
wisdom over innocence;
It's the descent from mesmerising
mirage into mystifying marsh.
It engenders a prolonged twilight;
The wisdom flares up in a flash,
Now, it's an enlightening darkness.

Missing Men

The census conveys concern
over the declining
Female to Male ratio;
Between the conception of
an exalted existence,
and the reality of
the social marginalization,
lie a few missing women, or
a few missing men?

Reflection

The symmetrical face,
The defined, sharp features,
The sparkling eyes,
Skin stretched in a tight sheen,
and flushed pink with passion,
The hair tossing wild and gay,
The frame a smiling blossom,
The bearing a buoyant sail;
Youth and beauty wedded into
the bliss of the prime!
Ah, mirror reveals the charm of youth!

The asymmetrical face-
an unfinished sculpture,
river fractured into delta,
The extinguishing eyes,
bags and crow-feet stealing the shape,
The jaw line collapsed into the neck,
The thinned hair-
the head a partially harvested field,
The frame a withering blossom,
The bearing a wading sail;
Age and hideousness huddled
into the agony of the decadence.
Oh, mirror impinges the ravages of age!

Sensibility surges into a sudden hiss,
do youth and beauty always breed bliss?
Narcissus looms large,
The terror of beauty takes charge;
The silvery waters beamed his beauty,
Hubris withered in youth his beauty.
Alas, ended his youth in youth!

Torn between revelation and impingement,
I sense a dewy blossom seared by drouth.

Confession of an Artist

Failures and frustration,
Compromises and consternation,
Regrets and remorse,
Sighs and sores,
suddenly come upon me
in a frightening heap,
Stark and searing;
Benumbing the senses,
Rendering me inert.

I reel under past's sway,
The soul again shows the way–
Surfeit of pain is pain no more,
Fear in excess is fortitude to the fore,
Take the bull by its horns
Pet the past, tame the thorns,
Articulate the agony,
Pen writes sighs as symphony.

In not long since I begin,
I feel the first quiver in the stone,
commences the catharsis,
rippling is set the stone!
Ah, happiness missed is ecstasy invented!

But what's this that impedes the flow,
and threatens to shadow the glow?

What when I use not mine
 but the pain that is thine?
A seeker of pain in the eternal
search for beauty;
An artist is a utilitarian who
trades his empathy for beauty.

Idol

A chance glance at the idol in the park,
as my racing car passes by;
I am severed from my surround;
It's a curious connection with my beloved deity.

Stirrings first, soulful sensations sweeping
over the being next;
The bright Sun setting a frozen lake
into a resplendent ripple,
Opening a morose Dahlia bud
into a bright, beaming blossom.

O Lord, oblivious to you I had been so long,
remained plunged into insentience prolonged!
But no later the wonder overtakes remorse,
A lifeless idol is this potent a force!

I am not a sage, nor a philosopher,
I can't comprehend in mind the eternity;
A simpleton, I rejoice at the idol's magic,
It is such an instant escort to eternity!

The Drought Is Born of Drought

The demon devastates;
Parched throats and burning bellies,
Steamy bosoms and muted screams,
Lifeless breath and deadening life.

"Nature yet again spews out a calamity,
The wrath is beyond man's wrap,"
A standard alibi is shot
to cock a snook at the rejected.

The drought is nourished upon
the mushrooming xerophytes,
They rule the roost,
The masters of the existent oases.

The mirage of the promises
delude the dying living,
They are fed upon the utopian dreams
by the dead living.

The drought devastates;
This demon is not a mythological import,
nor a nature's outcry,
The drought is born of Drought.

Air Is Morbid

Yet again, the same scene
at this square –
The hissing haze!
The furious fumes!
It simmers down to
the customary throngs of
the flashes and the sirens.

Floats to the fore the
scene seen just before –
Men exploded into parts many,
smeared in blood,
falling with a tormenting thud;
The macabre haze of
destruction and dust.

Strike awfully,
flanking the scene,
three huge hoardings-
They boasted of
a friendly health insurance,
a super specialty hospital, and
a new free health care policy.

I Seek God Not Religion

Approaching the temple, I stumble upon
thriving thieves and languishing lepers;
Asymmetry of a reconciled paradox,
How one revels and how one suffers.

I enter the temple, witness the
Sama of music and dance,
Devotees working frenziedly their ways
into a blissful trance.

Hopes fly thick and fast,
emanating from offerings and tears;
The reciprocity between faith and fullness;
Or propitiation out of mortal fears?

Mere chimera seems the Garden of Eden;
I know not what God is-Life's light real,
Or darkness beyond death,
Or a dialectical conception surreal.

No fullness, no transient trance,
No cure of even your mighty mystery;
I am capable of all comprehensions
but man's unfathomable asymmetry.

Oh, effect that void that is
equal to the flash of God,
Or leave me with my doubt,
and my religion without God.